Project Management Institute

Project Management Professional (PMP®) Examination Specification

ISBN: 1-930699-88-3

Published by: Project Management Institute, Inc.
Four Campus Boulevard
Newtown Square, Pennsylvania 19073-3299 USA
Phone: +610-356-4600
Fax: +610-356-4647
E-mail: pmihq@pmi.org
Internet: www.pmi.org

Table of Contents

Foreword

This *Project Management Professional (PMP®) Examination Specification (PMP Examination Specification™)* represents the most globally applicable, exhaustively researched, and legally defensible documentation of the tasks, knowledge, and skills demonstrated by project management practitioners. The *PMP Examination Specification* was developed through a global research study of the project management profession, known as a Role Delineation Study. The information contained herein is the culmination of valuable input on the part of dedicated volunteers from all areas of the globe.

The following pages contain the *PMP Examination Specification*. It includes an examination blueprint, which serves as the basis for creating the Project Management Professional (PMP) examination, an integral part of the requirements (along with education and experience) for earning the PMP credential.

By using the most effective and comprehensive methodology to define the roles and responsibilities of PMI-credentialed individuals, PMI will not only ensure that credentialed PMPs are truly worthy of the title, but that the PMP credential continues to attract qualified professionals. The results of this global study will serve to ensure the continued maturation of the project management profession on a global scale.

This undertaking would not have been possible without the hard work and dedication of PMI's volunteers and the overwhelming response of thousands in the project management field, worldwide, who took the time to fill out and return the comprehensive questionnaire. Their contribution to this *PMP Examination Specification*—and thereby to the future of the PMP credential and the overall project management profession—is monumental and deeply appreciated.

Cynthia McPherson, PMP
Chair, Certification Governance Council

Louis Mercken, MBA, PMP
2005 Chair – PMI Board of Directors

Preface

The Project Management Institute (PMI®) offers a professional credential known as the Project Management Professional (PMP®). PMI's professional credentialing examination development processes stand apart from other project management certification examination development practices, because PMI aligns its practices with the recognized international testing standard (ISO 17024) and the North American testing standards of the National Commission for Certifying Agencies (NCCA). One key component of the aforementioned standards is that organizations wishing to offer valid and reliable professional credentialing examinations are directed to use a job analysis, or role delineation study, as the basis for the creation of the examination. These processes provide best-practice guidelines for the credentialing organization to examine practitioners' tasks, and determine the level of importance, criticality, and frequency of each of these tasks. Conducting a study of this nature enables PMI to certify a candidate against the tasks deemed to be of utmost importance.

Through a global research study of the project management profession, known as a role delineation study, PMI developed this *PMP Examination Specification* from which PMI creates the credentialing examination. PMI continues to demonstrate and evolve its best-in-class examination development practices and as such often serves as a model for many other associations' professional credentials, since a study of this magnitude is rare, if at all seen, in the association professional credentialing world. PMPs can be confident that their professional credential has been developed according to best practices of test development standards. Please see Appendix A for a detailed description of the process.

Because the PMP examination is a vital part of the activities leading to one earning a professional credential, and because of PMI's goal to promote the profession through credentialed professionals, it is imperative that the PMP examination be a fair examination. Test content must reflect the knowledge and skills that individuals holding the PMP credential are expected to be able to demonstrate. All the questions and answers on the examination have been written and extensively reviewed by qualified PMPs and tracked to at least one project management reference. These questions are then mapped against the *PMP Examination Specification* to ensure that an appropriate number of questions are in place for a valid examination. In addition, qualified PMPs utilizing their professional judgment have determined the passing point of the examination through a certification industry standard process.

PMI retained CASTLE Worldwide, Inc. to conduct a global role delineation study. CASTLE is a professional testing company in Research Triangle Park, North Carolina, USA that specializes in the development and administration of licensure and certification examinations. CASTLE Worldwide, Inc. was also contracted to conduct the previous study, published by PMI in 2000. Since that time, the role of individuals pursuing the PMP has evolved in the marketplace, from that of managing deliverables across the five Project Management Process Groups, as defined in the *PMBOK® Guide*, to that of leading and directing project tasks. Based on these findings, the PMP credential requirements have been revised accordingly.

Please see the "PMP Certification Handbook" pdf for additional information on the application requirements. This electronic file is available through the "PMP Handbook" quick link under "Certifications" on PMI's Web site (www.pmi.org).

While the *PMP Examination Specification* and the *PMBOK® Guide*—Third Edition[1] naturally overlap, it is important to note that the individuals involved in the study described above were not bound by the *PMBOK® Guide*—Third Edition. They were charged with defining the role of individuals leading and directing project tasks, and using their experience and pertinent resources to help in this activity. Therefore, although many of the performance domains' tasks, knowledge, and skills outlined by the *PMP Examination Specification* are also covered by the *PMBOK® Guide*—Third Edition, there are some that are unique to the *PMP Examination Specification*. A notable difference is the performance domain entitled "Professional and Social Responsibility" in the *PMP Examination Specification*, which covers such aspects of the profession as legal, ethical, and professional behavior. The *PMBOK® Guide*—Third Edition does not explicitly address these issues, since this performance domain content relates to the individual, and the *PMBOK® Guide*—Third Edition relates to project management processes for a single project.

Candidates studying for the examination will certainly want to include the *PMBOK® Guide*—Third Edition as one of their study references, and would be well advised to read other contemporary resources on risk, scheduling, EVM, estimating, and other project management topics.

---

[1] *A Guide to the Project Management Body of Knowledge* (*PMBOK® Guide*)—Third Edition is recognized as the de facto global standard by the project management community. As a standard, it identifies and describes project management knowledge or practices that are applicable to projects. The *PMBOK® Guide*—Third Edition is the recognized reference source for anyone interested in the project management profession, and should be used to gain an understanding of project management knowledge that is needed to perform the Tasks described in the *PMP Examination Specification*.

Introduction

The *PMP Examination Specification* provides the basis for the PMP credentialing examination. Developed through a certification-industry standard practice, known as a Role Delineation Study, this *Examination Specification* provides the detail necessary for trainers to develop training materials, and serves as a guide to students as they focus their preparation studies.

The major function of the PMI credentialing program is to ensure competence and professionalism in the field of project management. Certification for individuals who lead and direct project tasks provides assurance that they have met specific criteria designed to ensure competence in the provision of services.

The development of a quality credentialing or licensing program must follow logically sound and legally defensible procedures based on psychometric literature and law. These principles and procedures are outlined in international standards such as ISO 17024 (*Conformity Assessment*—General Requirements for Bodies Operating Certification of Persons) and in federal regulation (*Uniform Guidelines on Employee Selection Procedures*) and manuals, such as *Standards for Educational and Psychological Testing* (published by the American Educational Research Association, 1999). PMI's credentialing examinations are developed with global processes aligned to these standards.

Before a content-valid examination is developed, the knowledge and skills necessary for competent practice in the profession must be determined. The process for identifying these competency areas is a role delineation, or job analysis, which serves as a blueprint for examination development. The role delineation also helps to determine the type of examination, such as written or practical, to be developed in order to assess competence.

The primary reason for conducting a role delineation study is to ensure the content validity of an examination. Content validity is the most commonly applied and accepted validation strategy for establishing certification programs today. In psychometric terms, validation is the way a test developer documents that the competence to be inferred from a test score is measured by the examination. A content-valid examination in project management, then, appropriately evaluates knowledge or skills required to function as a competent individual who leads and directs project tasks.

Thus, the role delineation study is an integral part of ensuring that an examination is content-valid and that the aspects of the project management profession covered on the examination reflect the tasks performed in practice settings. For both broad content areas and tasks, the study identified their importance, criticality, and frequency. These ratings play an important role in determining the content of the examination.

In the fall of 2004, four regional panels of project management experts assembled by the Project Management Institute (PMI) met with representatives of CASTLE Worldwide, Inc., to delineate the role of individuals who lead and direct project tasks. The panels met separately in San Francisco, Hong Kong, Frankfurt, and Buenos Aires to analyze this role in the four regions of the world; North America, Asia and the Pacific Rim, EMEA (Europe, Middle East, and Africa), and Central and South America, respectively. A fifth panel of experts met in Los Angeles to review the work of the four regional panels and to extract a single role delineation for global use. The fifth panel contained two representatives from each of the four regional panels, as well as individuals from each global region who had not participated in the earlier meetings.

Examination Specifications

The following examination specifications identify the proportion of questions from each domain that will appear on the examination and are derived by combining the overall evaluations of importance, criticality, and frequency, and converting the results into percentages. These percentages are used to determine the number of questions related to each domain and task that should appear on the multiple-choice format examination. The examination blueprint reflects the relative weightings/domain.

Examination Blueprint

Domain	Examination BLUEPRINT
	Survey Results Approximate Percentage of Items on Test
I. Initiating the Project	11%
II. Planning the Project	23%
III. Executing the Project	27%
IV. Monitoring and Controlling the Project	21%
V. Closing the Project	9%
VI. Professional and Social Responsibility	9%
Total	**100%**

Domains, Tasks, and Knowledge and Skill Statements

This section of the report contains the domains, tasks, and knowledge and skill statements as defined by the role delineation panels.

I.   Initiating the Project

II.   Planning the Project

III.   Executing the Project

IV.   Monitoring and Controlling the Project

V.   Closing the Project

VI..   Professional and Social Responsibility

Performance Domain I: Initiating the Project

Domain I	Initiating the Project—11%
Task 1	**Conduct project selection methods (e.g., cost benefit analysis, selection criteria) through meetings with the customer and experts, in order to evaluate the feasibility of new products or services.** Knowledge of: • Customer needs and expectations • Similar projects and/or areas • Organization's internal goals • Business environment • Presentation techniques • Approval procedure Skills in: • Active listening to the stakeholders and domain experts • Preparing a presentation that is well targeted to the audience • Communicating with the stakeholders and domain experts • Analysis and decision-making techniques • Analyzing cause and effect • Presenting the project vision to convince an audience
Task 2	**Define the scope of the project based on the business need, in order to meet the customer's project expectations.** Knowledge of: • Customer needs • Stakeholders' expectations • Historical information • Customer organizational structure Skills in: • Communicating • Interviewing stakeholders • Collecting historical information and lessons learned • Analysis and decision-making techniques
Task 3	**Document high-level risks, assumptions, and constraints using historical data and expert judgment, in order to understand project limitations.** Knowledge of: • Risk identification tools and techniques • Historical information • Estimation tools and techniques • Existing skills available in internal organization Skills in: • Identifying risk • Collecting historical information and lessons learned

(continued on next page)

(continued from previous page)

- Conducting estimates for budget, resource requirements, duration, and benefit
- Interviewing stakeholders
- Identifying assumptions and constraints
- Writing meaningful documents targeted to the planned audience

Task 4   **Perform key stakeholder analysis using brainstorming, organizational charts, interviewing techniques, and any available information, in order to gain buy-in and requirements for the success of the project.**

Knowledge of:
- Stakeholders
- Project objectives
- Organizational structure
- Brainstorming

Skills in:
- Identifying the requirements of stakeholders
- Aligning project objectives and stakeholders' requirements
- Stakeholder analysis techniques
- Brainstorming and interview techniques
- Facilitating
- Communicating with stakeholders

Task 5   **Develop the project charter through review with key stakeholders, in order to confirm project scope, risks, issues, assumptions, and constraints.**

Knowledge of:
- Development of the project charter
- Organizational templates
- Scope definition
- Risks, assumptions, and constraints
- Stakeholders

Skills in:
- Writing a synthetic and meaningful document targeted to the planned audience
- Creating a project charter
- Capturing and synthesizing primary information

Task 6   **Obtain project charter approval from the sponsor and customer (if required), in order to formalize authority, gain commitment, and project acceptance.**

Knowledge of:
- Project charter
- Organizational structure, policies, and procedures
- Approval process
- Presentation techniques

Skills in:
- Communicating
- Preparing a presentation
- Presenting the project vision to convince an audience

Performance Domain II: Planning the Project

Domain II	Planning the Project—23%
Task 1	**Record detailed customer requirements, constraints, and assumptions with stakeholders, in order to establish the project deliverables, using requirement-gathering techniques (e.g., planning sessions, brainstorming, focus groups) and the project charter.** Knowledge of: • Project charter • Configuration management system • Organizational structure, policies, and procedures • Stakeholders' expectations • Requirement gathering techniques Skills in: • Negotiating • Brainstorming • Role-playing • Facilitating • Documenting • Active listening • Interviewing • Building consensus
Task 2	**Identify key project team members by defining roles and responsibilities to create a project organization structure, in order to develop the communication plan.** Knowledge of: • Communication plan • Organizational structure • Stakeholders' expectations Skills in: • Documenting • Negotiating
Task 3	**Create the work breakdown structure with the team using appropriate tools and techniques, in order to develop the cost, schedule, resource, quality, and procurement plans.** Knowledge of: • Project charter • Work breakdown structure • Project deliverables • Organizational structure, policies, and procedures • Cost plan • Estimating techniques • Budgets

(continued on next page)

(continued from previous page)

- Schedule plan
- Network diagrams
- Simulation techniques
- Scheduling tools
- Resource plan
- Staffing requirements
- Stakeholder analysis
- Quality plan
- Acceptance criteria
- Quality processes and tools
- Procurement plan
- Service level agreements
- Solicitation plan

Skills in:
- Documenting
- Facilitating
- Negotiating
- Leading
- Prioritizing
- Budgeting
- Scheduling
- Estimating
- Dissimilating
- Collating

Task 4 **Develop the change management plan by defining how changes will be handled, in order to manage risk.**

Knowledge of:
- Scope
- Project deliverables
- Project requirements
- Configuration management
- Change management plan

Skills in:
- Negotiating
- Documenting
- Disseminating

Task 5 **Identify project risks by defining risk strategies and developing the risk management plan, in order to reduce uncertainty throughout the project life cycle.**

Knowledge of:
- Historical information
- Lessons learned
- Project charter
- Risk management plan
- Risk mitigation strategies and techniques

Skills in:
- Documenting
- Collating

(continued on next page)

(continued from previous page)

	• Forecasting • Quantifying • Disseminating
Task 6	**Obtain project plan approval from the customer, in order to formalize the project management approach.** Knowledge of: • Stakeholders' expectations • Acceptance criteria • Organizational structure, policies, and procedures Skills in: • Negotiating • Presenting • Influencing
Task 7	**Conduct a kick-off meeting with all key stakeholders, in order to announce the start of the project, and review the overall project plan and gain consensus.** Knowledge of: • Charter • Project plan • Organizational structure Skills in: • Presenting • Motivating

Performance Domain III: Executing the Project

Domain III	Executing the Project—27%
Task 1	**Execute the Tasks as defined in the project plan, in order to achieve the project goals.** Knowledge of: • Project plan • Statement of work • Configuration management • Procedures and company policies Skills in: • Leading • Coordinating
Task 2	**Ensure a common understanding by setting expectations in accordance with the project plan, in order to align the stakeholders and team members.** Knowledge of: • Project plan • Stakeholders' interests, expectations, and limitations Skills in: • Leading • Facilitating • Negotiating • Presenting
Task 3	**Implement the procurement of project resources in accordance with the procurement plan.** Knowledge of: • Procurement plan • Cost estimation tools and techniques • Contract administration • Organizational policies Skills in: • Negotiating • Analyzing
Task 4	**Manage resource allocation proactively by ensuring that appropriate resources and tools are assigned to the Tasks according to the project plan, in order to execute the planned Tasks successfully.** Knowledge of: • Project plan • Budget and time constraints • Organizational structure, culture, and policies Skills in: • Leading • Negotiating

(continued on next page)

(continued from previous page)

	<ul><li>Presenting</li><li>Problem solving</li></ul>
Task 5	**Implement the quality management plan to ensure that work is being performed according to required quality standards.** Knowledge of:<ul><li>Quality management plan</li><li>Scope, time, and cost constraints</li><li>Requirements specifications</li><li>Stakeholders' expectations</li></ul>Skills in:<ul><li>Auditing</li></ul>
Task 6	**Implement approved changes according to the change management plan, in order to ensure the successful completion and integration of all Tasks.** Knowledge of:<ul><li>Change management plan</li><li>Configuration management</li><li>"Triple constraint"</li></ul>Skills in:<ul><li>Communicating</li><li>Negotiating</li><li>Influencing</li><li>Documenting</li></ul>
Task 7	**Implement the approved actions and workarounds required to mitigate project risk events, in order to minimize the impact of the risks on the project.** Knowledge of:<ul><li>Risk management plan</li></ul>Skills in:<ul><li>Documenting</li></ul>
Task 8	**Improve team performance by building team cohesiveness, leading, mentoring, training, and motivating, in order to facilitate cooperation, ensure project efficiency, and boost morale.** Knowledge of:<ul><li>Organizational structure, policies, and procedures</li><li>Motivating factors</li><li>Team members' skill sets</li><li>Team members' interests</li></ul>Skills in:<ul><li>Leading</li><li>Facilitating</li><li>Negotiating</li><li>Motivating</li><li>Mentoring</li><li>Problem solving</li></ul>

Performance Domain IV: Monitoring and Controlling the Project

Domain IV	Monitoring and Controlling the Project—21%
Task 1	**Measure project performance using appropriate tools and techniques, in order to monitor the progress of the project, identify and quantify any variances, perform any required corrective actions, and communicate to all stakeholders.** Knowledge of: • Performance measuring and tracking techniques (e.g., EV, CPM, PERT, etc.) • Status reporting and distribution • Time management • Conflict resolution • Cost analysis • Project control limits (e.g., thresholds, tolerance) • Tools and metrics used throughout the project • Prioritization and decision-making techniques • Project templates and metrics • Variance and trend analysis Skills in: • Communicating to all stakeholders in a clear manner through appropriate channels and ensuring the correct interpretation of information • Problem solving regarding corrective actions to the identified variances • Analyzing and interpreting information and performance data • Implementing and encouraging corrective actions in a proactive way • Developing the root cause analysis
Task 2	**Manage changes to the project scope, project schedule, and project costs using appropriate verification techniques, in order to keep the project plan accurate, updated, reflective of authorized project changes as defined in the change management plan, and facilitate customer acceptance.** Knowledge of: • Integrated change control processes • Project templates and metrics (e.g., efforts, costs, milestones) • Project control limits (e.g., thresholds, tolerance) • Project plan management • Impact analysis Skills in: • Evaluating the impact of changes • Negotiating with stakeholders and getting approval from the change control board concerning changes in the project plan and necessary corrective actions • Communicating to all stakeholders in a clear manner through appropriate channels and ensuring the correct interpretation of information

(continued on next page)

(continued from previous page)

- Identifying and analyzing issues, in order to decide if changes to the project plan are required

Task 3 **Ensure that project deliverables conform to quality standards established in the project quality plan, using appropriate tools and techniques (e.g., testing, inspection, control charts), in order to adhere to customer requirements.**

Knowledge of:
- Quality planning and documentation
- Quality measurement tools (e.g., statistical sampling, control charts, flow-charting, inspection, etc.)
- Quality standards and conformance criteria
- Industry best practices and standards (e.g., ISO, BS, CMMI)
- Reporting procedures
- Process analysis
- Interviewing techniques

Skills in:
- Inspecting and reviewing
- Identifying and analyzing issues to ensure corrective actions
- Analyzing and elaborating on project reports
- Communicating to all stakeholders in a clear manner through appropriate channels and ensuring the correct interpretation of information
- Observing the process to capture deviations
- Active listening to create a friendly atmosphere in the workplace, in order to get information from team members regarding deviations
- Motivating and getting commitment related to quality standards

Task 4 **Monitor the status of all identified risks by identifying any new risks, taking corrective actions, and updating the risk response plan, in order to minimize the impact of the risks on the project.**

Knowledge of:
- Risk identification and analysis
- Risk response techniques (e.g., transference, mitigation, insurance, acceptance, etc.)
- Risk management planning
- Brainstorming
- Facilitation techniques
- Interviewing techniques

Skills in:
- Problem solving regarding the selection of alternative risk response strategies
- Negotiating with stakeholders and getting approval from the change control board regarding changes in the risk response plan and necessary corrective actions
- Communicating to all stakeholders in a clear manner through appropriate channels and ensuring the correct interpretation of information
- Using experience and expert judgment to identify risks and corrective actions
- Active listening to create a friendly atmosphere in the workplace, in order to get information from team members regarding risks

Performance Domain V: Closing the Project

Domain V	Closing the Project—9%
Task 1	**Formalize final acceptance for the project from the sponsor/customer by ensuring that the delivered product(s) and services comply with the agreed deliverables list, agreed scope, and any organizational procedures, in order to close contractual obligations and document the project's success.** Knowledge of: • Project scope • Deliverables • Acceptance criteria • Organizational structure, policies, and procedures • Contract and statutory requirements Skills in: • Negotiating • Presenting • Interviewing • Decision-making • Document writing • Managing conflict • Communicating
Task 2	**Obtain financial, legal, and administrative closure (e.g., final payments, warranties, contract signoff) for internal and external vendors and customers using generally accepted accounting practices and SOX compliance, in order to ensure no further expenditure and to communicate formal project closure.** Knowledge of: • Contract • Budgeting and expenditure processing • Conflict resolutions • Statutory requirements • Organizational policies and procedures Skills in: • Managing relationships • Negotiating • Communicating
Task 3	**Release all project resources using appropriate organizational policies and procedures (e.g., financial and human resources) and by providing performance feedback, in order to make them available for other future project assignments.** Knowledge of: • Organizational structure, policies, and procedures • Conflict resolution • Skills assessments

(continued on next page)

(continued from previous page)

- Team members and structure
- Performance metrics

Skills in:
- Coordinating
- Motivating
- Appraising
- Communicating

Task 4

Communicate lessons learned by means of ''post mortem'' team discussions, 360-degree surveys, supplier performance evaluations, and workshops, in order to create and/or maintain knowledge and experience that could be used in future projects, to improve overall project management processes, methodology, and decision-making, and to capitalize on best practices.

Knowledge of:
- Root-cause analysis techniques (e.g., fishbone/Ishikawa diagrams)
- Historical information
- Project scope and objectives
- Project contracts
- Stakeholders
- Industry best practices (e.g., CMM, CMMI, ISO)

Skills in:
- Document writing
- Objectivity
- Analyzing
- Presenting
- Communicating
- Facilitating

Task 5

Distribute the final project report using all project closure-related information, in order to highlight project variances, any open issues, lessons learned, and project deliverables, and to provide the final project status to all stakeholders.

Knowledge of:
- Organizational structure, policies, and procedures
- Archiving processes
- Project scope and deliverables
- Stakeholders

Skills in:
- Document/report writing
- Communicating
- Analyzing

Task 6

Archive project records, historical information, and documents (e.g., project schedule, project plan, lessons learned, surveys, risk and issues logs, etc.), in order to retain organizational knowledge, comply with statutory requirements, and ensure availability of data for potential use in future projects and internal/external audits.

Knowledge of:
- Organizational structure, policies, and procedures
- Archiving processes

(continued on next page)

(continued from previous page)

	• Project documents and records • Statutory requirements Skills in: • Document writing • Communicating
Task 7	**Measure customer satisfaction at the end of the project by capturing customer feedback using appropriate interview techniques and surveys, in order to gain, maintain, and improve customer long-term relationships.** Knowledge of: • Customer organizational structure • Stakeholders Skills in: • Interviewing • Communicating • Statistical sampling • Relationship building

Performance Domain VI: Professional and Social Responsibility

Domain VI	Professional and Social Responsibility—9%
Task 1	**Ensure personal integrity and professionalism by adhering to legal requirements, ethical standards, and social norms, in order to protect the community and all stakeholders and to create a healthy working environment.** Knowledge of: • Legal requirements • Ethical standards • Social norms • Community and stakeholder values • Communication techniques Skills in: • Exercising judgment • Researching law and regulation, ethical standards, organizational and stakeholder values, and social norms • Gathering, assessing, compiling, and documenting information • Negotiating effectively • Resolving conflicts • Communicating effectively
Task 2	**Contribute to the project management knowledge base by sharing lessons learned, best practices, research, etc., within appropriate communities, in order to improve the quality of project management services, build the capabilities of colleagues, and advance the profession.** Knowledge of: • The project management body of knowledge • Effective communication techniques • Techniques for transferring knowledge • Research techniques Skills in: • Communicating effectively • Exercising judgment • Transferring knowledge (coaching, mentoring, training, etc.) • Implementing research techniques • Gathering, assessing, compiling, and documenting information
Task 3	**Enhance personal professional competence by increasing and applying knowledge, in order to improve project management services.** Knowledge of: • Personal strengths and weaknesses • Instructional methods and tools • Appropriate professional competencies

(continued on next page)

(continued from previous page)

- Training options
- Self-assessment strategies

Skills in:
- Planning personal development
- Attaining and applying new project management practices
- Communicating effectively

Task 4   **Promote interaction among team members and other stakeholders in a professional and cooperative manner by respecting personal and cultural differences, in order to ensure a collaborative project management environment.**

Knowledge of:
- Interpersonal techniques
- Cultural differences
- Community and stakeholder values
- Communication techniques
- Team motivation strategies

Skills in:
- Exercising judgment
- Researching organizational and stakeholder values
- Gathering, assessing, compiling, and documenting information
- Negotiating effectively
- Resolving conflicts
- Communicating effectively
- Respecting cultural differences
- Motivating teams

Appendix A:

Process to Develop the PMP Examination

Defining the Responsibilities

The first step in developing a certification examination is to define the responsibilities of the recipients of the credential. It must be known what individuals who lead and direct project tasks actually do on the job *before* a content-valid test can be developed. A content-valid examination draws questions from every important area of the profession and specifies that performance areas (domains) considered more important, critical, and relevant be represented by more questions on the examination. Defining the role of individuals leading and directing project tasks occurs in two major phases: one in which individuals currently in the role define the responsibilities, and another in which the identified responsibilities are validated on a global scale.

In the second half of 2004, a series of international meetings sponsored by PMI was held in the four major regions of the world (as currently defined by PMI): EMEA (Europe, Middle East, and Africa), Asia-Pacific, Latin America, and North America. The meetings involved panels of global project management practitioners who met to develop a comprehensive description of the Tasks that individuals leading and directing project tasks perform. These regional meetings were followed by a final meeting at Global Congress 2004—North America, where the final list of Tasks was agreed upon by a group of panelists from around the world.

Panel participants, working under the direction of CASTLE, reached consensus on the performance domains, a broad category of duties and responsibilities that define the role. The panelists identified six domains that are important for competent performance by an individual who leads and directs project tasks:

- Initiating the Project

- Planning the Project

- Executing the Project

- Monitoring and Controlling the Project

- Closing the Project

- Professional and Social Responsibility.

Next, panelists defined the Tasks that are important for each domain, along with statements about the knowledge and skills that are associated with performing each Task competently.

Validating the Responsibilities Identified by the Panelists

In order to ensure the validity of the study and content outline developed by the panels, a survey requesting feedback on the panel's work was sent to project management practitioners throughout the world. Surveys were distributed globally to thousands of people from 78 countries, with a robust response rate, indicating an extremely high return rate for a survey of this type and providing PMI the statistical significance from which to draw conclusions about the importance, criticality, and frequency of the Tasks.

Survey respondents evaluated the domains and Tasks identified by the panelists by evaluating their importance, criticality and frequency on a five-point Likert-type scale:

- Importance—degree to which it is essential to be competent in the domain or Task, in order to provide competent service;

- Criticality—degree to which incompetence in the domain or Task could bring about harm;

- Frequency—percent of projects on which duties were performed, associated with each domain.

Developing a Plan for the Test

Based on respondent ratings, an examination blueprint, clarifying exactly how many questions from each domain and Task should be on the examination, was developed. Those domains and Tasks that were rated as most important, critical and relevant by survey respondents would have the most questions devoted to them on the examination.

Another aspect of PMI's leading-edge examination development practices is introducing an enhanced examination development activity. *Pretest* questions will be randomly placed throughout the new examination to gather statistical information on the performance of these questions, in order to determine whether they may be used on future examinations. These 25 pretest items are included in the 200-question examination, but will not be included in the pass/fail determination; candidates will be scored on 175 questions. The pretest items will allow PMI to monitor the question performance better, prior to including the questions in the final databank of test questions.

Results of the study indicated that the 175 scoreable questions on the test should be distributed among the domains as shown in the below table. As previously noted, the remaining 25 questions will be disbursed throughout the domains as pretest questions and will not count in candidates' scores.

Domains	% of Items / Domain
I. Initiating the Project	11
II. Planning the Project	23
III. Executing the Project	27
IV. Monitoring and Controlling the Project	21
V. Closing the Project	9
VI. Professional Responsibility	9
	100%

Number of Questions

Number of Scoreable Questions	175
Pretest Questions	25
Total	200